Cambridge E

T0277430

Elements in the Pro
edited by
Michael L. Peterson
Asbury Theological Seminary

GOD AND POLITICAL THEORY

Tyler Dalton McNabb
Saint Francis University

Shaftesbury Road, Cambridge CB2 8EA, United Kingdom

One Liberty Plaza, 20th Floor, New York, NY 10006, USA

477 Williamstown Road, Port Melbourne, VIC 3207, Australia

314–321, 3rd Floor, Plot 3, Splendor Forum, Jasola District Centre, New Delhi – 110025, India

103 Penang Road, #05–06/07, Visioncrest Commercial, Singapore 238467

Cambridge University Press is part of Cambridge University Press & Assessment, a department of the University of Cambridge.

We share the University's mission to contribute to society through the pursuit of education, learning and research at the highest international levels of excellence.

www.cambridge.org
Information on this title: www.cambridge.org/9781009269100

DOI: 10.1017/9781009269117

© Tyler Dalton McNabb 2022

First published 2022

A catalogue record for this publication is available from the British Library.

ISBN 978-1-009-26910-0 Paperback
ISSN 2754-8724 (online)
ISSN 2754-8716 (print)

God and Political Theory

Elements in the Problems of God

DOI: 10.1017/9781009269117
First published online: November 2022

Tyler Dalton McNabb
Saint Francis University

Author for correspondence: Tyler Dalton McNabb, TMcNabb@Francis.edu

Abstract: How is God related to the state? Could the existence of robust political authority somehow be evidence for God? In this Element, the author explores these questions, pro and con, looking at various major positions. At the start of the Element, he defends a political argument for God's existence. Having motivated a theistic account of political authority, he then discusses the role God plays or could play in classical liberalism, Marxism, and postliberalism. While he sympathetically surveys each political theory in turn, at the end of each section, he raises diverse objections to the view being discussed. Finally, at the end of the Element, the author articulates desiderata for theists who are looking for political frameworks.

Keywords: Huemer, social contract, natural law, political authority, liberalism

ISBNs: 9781009269100 (PB), 9781009269117 (OC)
ISSNs: 2754-8724 (online), 2754-8716 (print)

Contents

1 Grounding Political Authority

1.1 Political Authority

Imagine that you are walking in a dark alley and a man comes up to you with a gun and yells out, "Give me your money!" You would think that you are being robbed. Perhaps you would give your money over to the man in the hope that he would spare your life. But you would think that this man has no right to it. Let's call this Scenario 1 (S1).

Let's replay this scenario but, instead of a random man with a gun, let's say that representatives of your state come knocking on your door.[1] You open the door and invite them in. They quickly inform you that you didn't pay enough taxes and that you owe the state additional money. Now, you might be taken aback and you might hate that you were off on your calculations. Nonetheless, you pay up as you think you owe the state more money. Let's call this Scenario 2 (S2).

Is there a moral difference between S1 and S2? Or are the state's representatives in S2 no different than a common thief? Contra the popular libertarian mantra, taxation is not theft. The difference between S1 and S2 relates to the nature of authority. The thief in S1 lacks authority to force you to give up your wallet while the state has legitimate claim over at least some of your funds. Specifically, the state has the right to create tax revenue from its citizens and from it provide services such as food and healthcare for those in need. But the state doesn't just have the authority to do this. The state has what I call robust authority. The state can also use those tax dollars to develop infrastructure, educate its citizens, fund space programs, develop the arts, and provide a culture for its citizens. Of course, a legitimate state can also enforce bans, protect its borders, and imprison transgressors. The state can regulate trade and declare just wars.

Now, one might think that there is a limit to what a state can do. For example, you might think that the state can't violate a citizen's right to wear a hijab or prevent a father from defending the lives of his innocent children. Nonetheless, when I reflect on the relationship between a state and its citizens, it seems to me that states possess robust political authority over their citizens.

Perhaps you're thinking, "Is that all your evidence for thinking a state possesses robust authority? I thought philosophers were supposed to make cases for what they believe. Does your case for robust political authority really reduce to the simple fact that it seems to you to be the case?"

---

[1] By state, I don't mean to include just our contemporary and relatively recent understanding of nation-states. Rather, I want to include ancient conceptions of the state as well. See Sandeford (2018).

Maybe you're not even there yet. You could have become convinced by an extremely reductionistic view of the world that states don't even exist, at least as agents that aren't reducible to some collection of individuals. Rather, you think that we act as if the state is real because it allows us to easily talk about which collection of agents possesses power and which collection of agents is responsible for various actions.

What can I say to convince you that your possible skepticism is misplaced? First, let me tell you that your expectation for philosophers is too high. Philosophers usually believe what they believe because it's what all the other fashionable philosophers believe. Sorry to disappoint. Appealing to what appears to be the case, then, seems not so bad. In fact, a good number of epistemologists argue that a subject, S, can have a justified belief, P, if it seems to S that P, and S is without a defeater for her belief that P.[2]

We can call those experiences that incline us to believe in propositions, seemings.[3] Seemings are evidence for propositions and often they are the only good evidence we have. Take S's belief that other minds exist as an example. How is S's belief justified? Is it by some argument? Not likely. S most likely came to believe that other minds exist not by way of inference, but in an immediate way. From coming into contact with other minds, S's faculties produce a strong experience that leads her to believe that other minds exist.[4]

Do not think that this strong experience is sufficient for her belief to be justified. You might be in for some epistemic trouble. As Alvin Plantinga has pointed out, the arguments for other minds aren't too impressive.[5] Perhaps the best argument for other minds goes something like this:

> Let's say that S opens her front door and sees what appears to her to be a group of people. We should treat S's belief that a group of people stand before her, as a hypothesis. Specifically, we can call this the Group hypothesis. How do we know that the Group hypothesis is explanatorily better off than those competing hypotheses that reject the existence of this group? You might say that S postulating the existence of a group makes sense of her seeming. Moreover, you might think that the Group hypothesis is a simpler hypothesis than alternative hypotheses, such as, the group of individuals are actually well-designed robots that have been secretly put together by the US government. So, S's belief that a group of people are in front of her is probably justified by way of inference to the best explanation.

---

[2] Those who endorse this thesis advocate what is known as phenomenal conservativism. See chapter 5 of Huemer (2001).

[3] Here I follow Michael Bergmann (2002) in giving a minimalist definition of a seeming.

[4] Assuming that her cognitive faculties are working properly, it would seem that her belief would also possess warrant. See McNabb (2018).

[5] For a survey of such arguments, see Plantinga (1993, pp. 69–71).

What exactly is the problem with this argument? For starters, it isn't clear to me that S's Group hypothesis is all that simple. Wouldn't it be simpler for S to explain her seeming by way of postulating that only she and a Cartesian demon exist and that her seeming is the result of the demon's clever tricks? No need to postulate a group of minds, or more than 7 billion of them, for that matter (this isn't even taking into account extraterrestrial life). Or she might postulate that only she exists and her belief that other minds exist is the result of hallucinations. These seem like simpler alternatives.

Let's say that the argument has more going for it than meets the eye. Perhaps the argument is simpler than the alternatives I've brought up. How much simpler would it be? Does an inference to the best explanation really capture the degree of justification we think we have for our belief that other minds exist? What do we do with younger children who believe that other minds exist? Do young children come by their beliefs by way of justified inferences? If not, are we to say that their beliefs relating to other persons are not justified? This all seems rather implausible.

Of course, we can avoid all this talk about best explanation and meeting some hard evidential standard of rationality if we simply permit seemings to count as sufficient evidence for our beliefs. I think I'm on good ground, then, to utilize seemings when discussing justification as it relates to political authority.

Enough epistemology. Why think that states are real entities and not useful fictions that help explain power dynamics? Well, it sure seems to me that states are genuine agents that are not reducible to those members that constitute them.[6] Simply put, it seems to me that states are non-reducible entities for which our ontology should make room. But do states possess robust authority over their citizens? Again, it sure seems to me that states have the right to tax their citizens so that states can guarantee their citizens' safety, healthcare, education, and so on. So, we have evidence for thinking that states exist and they possess robust political authority. We can call this thesis the state realist thesis (SRT).

In this section, I assume SRT (apologies in advance to my readers who don't like "seeming" talk). With this assumption stated, I argue that secular accounts of political authority (accounts from below) ultimately are explanatorily weaker than a theistic account of political authority. This not only gives us reason to endorse a theistic account over competing secular accounts. It also provides evidence for theism.

Having defended giving God a large role in overall political theory, I turn in Sections 2–4 to the role God plays or could play in the following philosophical frameworks: classical liberalism, Marxism, and postliberalism.

---

[6] For arguments for realist views of collective agency, see Tollefsen (2007).

While I sympathetically survey each political theory in turn, at the end of each section, I also provide what I find to be the most pressing problems for each political framework. While my criticisms do not solely relate to how a theist should think about political philosophy, this concern is driving much of what I have to say in this Element. Finally, I end the Element by discussing what theists should be looking for in political frameworks.

1.2 Contractarianism

Traditional social contract theory (TSCT) is roughly the thesis that, when entities agree on how they should socially interact, normative properties emerge from the agreement.[7] That is, on the basis of their agreement, the entities in question obtain duties with respect to how they should behave toward each other. For example, if S1 agrees to give up her natural right to φ on the condition that S2 will provide services to her, S1 and S2 now have duties to not violate their agreement. I now explicate the finer details of TSCT by way of situating the theory in the historical figures of Plato and John Locke.

In *Crito*, we find Socrates patiently awaiting his execution. While Socrates seems content with his conviction, his friend Crito comes to help him escape. Socrates isn't persuaded to leave, however. Instead, Socrates lectures Crito about why he ought to obey the state and go through with the execution. Socrates' primary justification for why he ought to obey his government is that he has made an agreement or contract with the Athenian government.[8] By choosing to live in Athens, he has consented to the authority of Athens' government. Since he freely entered into this contract, it would be unjust to violate it.

In the seventeenth century, the English philosopher John Locke explicated this idea more thoroughly. For Locke, historically speaking, a legitimate state is created when in the state of nature, a group of individuals collectively consent to each other (Locke, 1988). The members of the group freely give up some of their natural rights for various protections. We can say that a contract is made between the group of individuals.

While this might explain how the state came into existence, we might wonder why those who were not a part of the original agreement must obey the state. For instance, let's say that two of the members of the original group have a child together. We can call this child Tim. Why should Tim obey the state? Tim wasn't there when the original agreement was made, nor has Tim ever explicitly consented to the state.

---

[7] This definition is roughly the definition found in D'Agostino and Gaus (2021).
[8] See *Crito* 51c–53a.

In response to this question, Locke developed the theory of tacit or implicit consent.[9] Roughly, the idea is that while Tim has never explicitly consented to the state, nonetheless, by utilizing the resources of the state, such as highways, Tim gives implicit consent to the state. The idea of implicit consent shouldn't seem too foreign to us. We give implicit consent every time we order food at a restaurant. That is, by ordering food we are implicitly consenting to pay for it. Similarly, there are gas stations where you pump your gas before you pay. You sign no contract obligating you to pay for the gas, but, by taking the gas, you are implicitly consenting to pay for it.

Having explicated TSCT, we are now in the position to critically evaluate it.[10] We begin with Michael Huemer's critiques of TSCT. Specifically, Huemer points out that, in order for a contract to be valid, the following four conditions must be met:

(1) Valid consent requires a reasonable way of opting out.
(2) Explicit dissent trumps alleged implicit consent.
(3) An action can be taken as indicating agreement to some scheme only if we can assume that, if we did not take that action, the scheme would not be imposed upon us.
(4) Contractual obligation is mutual and conditional. (Huemer, 2013, p. 25)

Regarding (1), Huemer gives an example of a chairman who asks his colleagues to do something unreasonable in order to avoid their next scheduled meeting. Namely, he asks his colleagues to cut off their left arms if they don't want to meet at the allotted time (Huemer, 2013, p. 25). Clearly, there would not be many takers. While it is the case that the chairman gives a way to opt out of the next business meeting – you can even picture the chairman reminding his employees that he gave them a choice – this in no way should be considered a valid agreement as there is no reasonable way to opt out.

Huemer makes (2) plausible, utilizing a typical transaction at a restaurant as an example (Huemer, 2013, p. 26). Typically, when you walk into a restaurant and order food, there is an implicit contract made between you and the server. Namely, by ordering the food, you are agreeing to pay for it. Now, let's say that you walk into your favorite restaurant and order your favorite meal. Unlike under normal circumstances, however, after ordering, you inform the server that you will not be paying for the food today. If the server still brings you the food, it seems like you are no longer obligated to pay for it. Your explicit dissent makes the contract no longer valid.

---

[9] See Locke (1988), especially 2.122.
[10] I also discuss this (though less thoroughly) in Neill and McNabb (2019).

Regarding (3), Huemer again brings up the uncaring chairman, who now informs his employees that, no matter what anyone says, there will be a meeting at some specific time, let's say next Monday at 12 p.m. He then asks his employees to dissent if they don't want to have a meeting at that specific time. Even if no one dissents, it seems implausible that his employees agreed to meet next week (Huemer, 2013, p. 26). Finally, with respect to (4), "A contract normally places both parties under an obligation to each other, and one party's rejection of his contractual obligation releases the other party from her obligation" (p. 27). There isn't much to explain here. If you sign a contract with a landlord that states that you will pay money to the landlord, if the landlord lets you live in his home, then you owe the landlord rent only if he allows you to live in his home. If the landlord kicks you out, you are no longer obligated to pay him rent.

All of Huemer's conditions for a valid contract are plausible. And I'm not aware of any good counterexample to his criteria. So, let's assume that Huemer is right. What follows for TSCT? Well, it follows that, in most circumstances, TSCT would lack the tools to make sense of robust political authority. For example, as Huemer states, there's typically no reasonable way for a citizen to opt out of a contract with the state:

> To leave one's country, one must generally secure the permission of some other state to enter its territory, and most states impose restrictions on immigration. In addition, some individuals lack the financial resources to move to the country of their choice. Those who can move may fail to do so due to attachments to family, friends, and home. Finally, if one moves to another country, one will merely become subject to another government.
>
> (pp. 29–30)

Moreover, as Huemer notes, TSCT can't show that the state has robust political authority over explicit dissenters. Anarchists would be in an analogous position to the customer who informs her server that she will not pay for her meal but will happily receive the food if it comes out. A plausible account of political authority needs to account for why the state has authority over explicit dissenters.

Now, let's say you're sold on TSCT not working. What about other contractarian theories such as a standard hypothetical social contract theory (HSCT)? Generally, a proponent of HSCT concedes that, on average, the state doesn't derive its authority from an explicit or implicit agreement with its citizens. Rather, the state's authority is analogous to a doctor's authority when the doctor is working on an unconscious patient. It's assumed that, hypothetically, if the patient were conscious, she would ask the doctor to operate on her. Given the likely truth of this counterfactual, the doctor is justified with respect to operating on an unconscious patient. The doctor has coercive authority over his patient. In the same way, if S was offered a contract with the state, she would likely make an agreement with the state. So, the state has legitimate coercive authority over S.

Now, I don't doubt that many people, in fact, the vast majority, would indeed give consent to a contract with the state if the alternative was some Hobbesian state of nature. However, there would still be a minority who would reject such a contract. Here, I especially have in mind philosophical anarchists such as Huemer, although there are other exceptions.

Now, as Huemer points out, many think it would be immoral for the doctor to operate on the patient if she was conscious and refused to give the doctor permission to operate on her. This is more analogous to the situation of those who explicitly dissent from the state (Huemer, 2013, p. 94). Anarchists are, for example, conscious. Yet they actively refuse and protest the state's authority. Are we to assume, then, that the state is violating the rights of anarchists just as the doctor violates the rights of his patient? This seems implausible. Regardless of what the anarchists think, the state has robust authority over them. Like our moral duties, the state possessing authority over S depends in no way on what S thinks about the state.

1.3 Consequentialism

For these reasons, contractarian accounts generally fail to make sense of how a state has robust political authority. More promising are consequentialist accounts. Here's a standard consequentialist account: State ST can rightfully coerce a set of persons, SP, if, by not coercing SP, catastrophic consequences would occur.

In order to bring intuitive force to us, his readers, on behalf of the consequentialist, Huemer invites us to imagine being on a sinking lifeboat. We correctly conclude that, if everyone doesn't start bailing, the boat will sink, resulting in the deaths of all on board (Huemer, 2013, p. 94). We can even spice up Huemer's thought experiment and imagine that there are small children on board who will also die if those onboard do not heed our warning. Imagine now that no one on the lifeboat takes us seriously and everyone proceeds to act as if everything is normal. Let's also say that we happen to carry guns (perhaps we are from Texas). Might we be justified if we used them in a threatening way and ordered everyone to bail? Consequentialists think we would be. But where does this lead us? Is this a plausible account of political authority?

First, I'm not yet convinced that consequentialist accounts are genuine accounts of political authority. Let's go back to the bailing scenario. In this scenario, do we really have authority over everyone in the boat? It's not clear to me that we do. Now, this isn't to say that we aren't justified in threatening our comrades in order to save everyone on the boat. The bailing scenario is primarily showing that we can permissibly coerce individuals even when we don't have genuine authority over them. Typically, we understand that coercion is justified only in circumstances where we have genuine authority. Scenarios like this show us that there are cases where we lack genuine authority but coercion is still permissible. In this way, the state might not have genuine authority over you, but it would be justified in coercing your behavior.

Let's say that I'm thinking about this all wrong and, in fact, the bailing scenario shows that states do possess genuine political authority. I'm still not inclined to think that the consequentialist gives us a plausible account of *robust* political authority. That is, it might show us that the state has the right to protect life and the environment, given that life and the environment would be in immediate danger of annihilation if the state didn't utilize coercion against relevant subjects. But it wouldn't show that the state has the right to make and enforce laws regulating marriage, space exploration, government schools, large welfare programs, minimum wage laws, laws that prohibit immoral behavior, and laws that prohibit people from harming themselves (Huemer, 2013, pp. 95–96). The bailing scenario only moves us because without the coercion, there is immediate and clear catastrophic danger. Laws that prohibit immoral behavior and expand our knowledge of the cosmos don't seem to be in the same boat (pun intended) as the catastrophes that would occur if the state stopped enforcing laws relating to murder and rape.

1.4 Naturalism and Natural Law

So, if we are after naturalistic accounts of robust political authority, I think, again, we must go elsewhere. While most of my analytic readers familiar with the state of contemporary political philosophy might be all out of ideas, here is another proposal that we should consider.[11]

Natural law theory is made up of two tenets: (1) Morality is objective. (2) Morality is derived from human nature.[12] In the Thomistic tradition, flowing

---

[11] I only have so much space to engage various accounts of political authority. I decided to engage accounts that to me offer the best hope for securing a secular account of robust political authority. But I do want to let the reader know that other accounts are indeed offered in the literature (other accounts that seem ultimately unsuccessful to me). See Dworkin (1986) and Waldron (1999).

[12] What is described in what follows falls into the category of traditional natural law theory. Traditional natural law assumes controversial metaphysical views. For an interpretation of natural law that does not utilize robust metaphysics, see Finnis (2011).

from the relevant form, the human person possesses parts and these parts possess teleology.[13] Specifically, each part possesses at least one end. Understanding a part's end can help us to understand how the idealized human person should operate. For example, a subject's heart should be pumping blood and her ears should be hearing the sounds that surround her. We can of course further explore the idealized human person. She would have arms that hold up objects. She would have legs that get her from one place to another. And she would of course have a mouth that conveys truths and a brain that helps her become aware of her surroundings.

These parts, then, have design plans that determine how the parts and the body should be used in order for the subject to flourish. She needs these parts to function properly. It would then be bad if a subject intentionally prevented a part from achieving its end by way of doing something contrary to that part's end.[14] Both the part and the individual subject could no longer be said to be flourishing, at least according to idealized human nature.

Now, according to the Aristotelian–Thomistic natural law tradition, teleology is not only essential to the human person. As humans are political animals, teleology is also essential to political philosophy (Miller). Humans are also social animals and depend on other social animals for their own flourishing. Humans, then, also require a state to organize those relationships. The state can be said to be natural to our human nature or even teleologically required by it.

If one is committed to developing a purely naturalistic or secular account of natural law, I have a hard time seeing how all of this is supposed to work out. Specifically, I have a hard time understanding how to make sense of human nature being highly teleological on purely naturalistic grounds.[15]

Not all naturalist share my seeming, of course. A naturalist might argue that we can derive objective norms from the nature of organisms, specifically by understanding what is good and what is bad for the organisms in question. Elsewhere, Erik Baldwin and I summarize a proper function account inspired by Philippa Foot:[16]

(1) Organisms (and their organs), including humans, have natural functions, and facts about the natural functions of organisms, together with facts about

---

[13] For an analysis of Thomas Aquinas' mereology and for an explanation for how parts possess teleology, see Salzillo (2021).

[14] For more on this, see Hsiao (2017) and Skalko (2019).

[15] Perhaps a panpsychist will have a better time than a materialist in making sense of teleology, but there are, of course, reasons why panpsychism has failed to dominate analytic Western philosophy of mind. See, for example, Plantinga's (2012) critique.

[16] For Foot's account, see Foot (2002).

the natural environments in which they arise and thrive, determine the objective standards of natural goodness of humans (and their organs).

(2) If there are objective standards of natural goodness for humans, then there are objective natural norms that specify the criteria of appropriate or proper function for humans.

(3) There are objective standards of natural goodness for humans (and their organs).

Thus,

(4) There are objective natural norms that specify the criteria of appropriate or proper function for human organisms (and their organs). [From (1) to (3)]

(5) If there are objective natural norms that specify the criteria for the proper function of human organisms (and their organs), then Neo-Aristotelians (and like-minded others who recognize these facts, too) can make sense of the proper function of parts.

Thus,

(6) Neo-Aristotelians (and like-minded others who recognize these facts, too) can make sense of the proper function of parts. [From (4) to (5)].[17]

Let's first look at (1) in more detail. On naturalism, why think that organisms possess functions? Thinking that organisms possess functions on naturalism becomes even less obvious if we understand functions, as I have articulated, as interchangeable with design plans (Plantinga, 1993). I grant that on naturalism it might look like the parts that make up human beings (e.g., arms) have design plans, but it's more likely that the appearance of design plans is illusionary and is the result of natural selection. It simply seems to me (and I imagine to many others) that genuine design plans require agents or designers (or something like them). For natural law theory to make sense, then, we need to invoke God. This point is a familiar one to those who follow Aquinas and his 5th Way.[18] For further reasons as to why naturalistic accounts of design plans and proper function don't work, see my work with Baldwin that argues that naturalistic accounts don't supply necessary and sufficient conditions for proper function.[19]

Finally, it's important to note that natural law proponents will always have to deal with what is known as the is-ought fallacy. As David Hume puts it,

---

[17] This has been slightly edited for contextual reasons. See Baldwin and McNabb (2018, pp. 37–38).

[18] For Thomas' argument, see *Summa Theologica*, Part 1, Question 2. For a contemporary defense, see Feser (2009).

[19] Feser (2009, pp. 29–42).

[W]hen of a sudden I am surprised to find, that instead of the usual copulations of propositions, is, and is not, I meet with no proposition that is not connected with an ought, or an ought not. This change is imperceptible; but is, however, of the last consequence. For as this ought, or ought not, expresses some new relation or affirmation, it is necessary that it should be observed and explained; and at the same time that a reason should be given, for what seems altogether inconceivable, how this new relation can be a deduction from others, which are entirely different from it. (Hume, 2009, p. 715)

Roughly, the idea is that you can't derive normativity from a descriptive analysis – in this case, human nature. Just because S is the sort of creature that would flourish by obeying the state, it doesn't follow that S ought to obey the state. Typically, natural law theorists have an assumption that flourishing is good and that, in order to flourish, we should perform those actions that enable us to do so. I don't think Hume would be impressed. Why ought we to do those actions that enable us to flourish? Why is it that flourishing is good? This Element is an introductory work meant to provoke more questions than it answers. While I am by no means arguing that naturalists are without a response, these are important issues to highlight.

1.5 Wolterstorff's Accounts from Above and Below

In light of these criticisms, I now invite the reader to consider a theistic account of political authority. Following the Christian tradition, Nicholas Wolterstorff argues that God grounds political authority.[20] God possesses authority over all mankind such that He can rightfully grant states the right to govern people.[21] Out of God's love for shalom and His desire for injustices to dissipate, God gives authority the state "to exercise governance over the public so as to curb wrongdoing." Wolterstorff states that "When the state acts for the purpose of curbing injustice in society, its directives are binding; they generate in the public the obligation to obey" (Wolterstorff, 2012b, p. 113).

Wolterstorff does a study on the word *shalom* and concludes that God gives authority to the state to not only protect rights and enforce contracts but also to "build infrastructure, secure coordination of activities, [and] find and maintain institutions and landscapes that are of public benefit" (p. 114).[22] The authority God that grants the state is clearly robust.

---

[20] See Wisdom 6 and Romans 13.

[21] You might be wondering what my justification is for thinking that God has authority over all humans. Well, I'm sorry to disappoint, but it just seems obvious to me that, if God exists, He'd have authority over His creation and He could delegate as He sees fit. I think the seeming that leads me to believe this is likely shared by the vast majority of humans who have ever existed. If this doesn't satisfy you, perhaps you should look at Murphy (2017).

[22] I've made a very slight edit to this quote in order for it to match the relevant grammar.

It's interesting to note, however, that Wolterstorff thinks that God grants states what he calls performance authority over and against what he calls positional authority. Positional authority is authority that is ultimate. It is authority that overrides all other moral duties. If a state tells its citizens to worship Baal, the citizens ought to worship Baal because the state said so. Performance authority, on the other hand, is authority that the state could have taken away if, for example, the state fails to bring shalom to its people (p. 115). Readers familiar with traditional Chinese philosophy will see the similarities between Wolterstorff's performance account of authority and the doctrine of the Mandate of Heaven. In both cases, Divinity gives its approval to a ruler and if the ruler fails in his duties, Divinity gives the mandate to govern to another.

Wolterstorff's account from "above" can be contrasted with his political authority account from "below." Wolterstorff endorses overdetermination with respect to political authority. Not only is there a theistic grounding of political authority; there is also a purely secular justification for political authority as well. Wolterstoff is not too high on contemporary secular accounts of political authority, but, as you might have gathered, Wolterstorff thinks his secular account has something going for it.

Roughly, the idea goes as follows: Humans have rights. We have the right to not be gravely harmed. Moreover, we have the right to have a higher institution protect us. As Wolterstorff puts it, we have a right to "some institutionalized arrangement for protecting us against being seriously wronged by our fellows" (Wolterstorff, 2012a, p. 275). So this higher institution can rightfully coerce relevant persons as it carries out its task to adjudicate justice. Of course, this account doesn't tell us anything about if this institution has the right to tax those under its jurisdiction and, if so, if there is some limit. Nor can Wolterstorff's theory make sense of how the state has robust political authority, unless one wants to say that humans possess the right for the state to fund the arts, sponsor space exploration, and update infrastructure. That seems a bit too much to bite off. Wolterstorff of course acknowledges this when he states the following:

> The sketch just presented, of an account from below of the political authority of the state, says nothing about the status of those legislative enactments that are aimed not at protecting citizens against serious violations of their right by other citizens but at bringing about some common good – for example, a bill for the construction of highways and for the imposition of taxes to support that construction. Either legislation does not generate obligations in citizens, or if it does, accounting for why it does will need to take a quite different form from the account of political obligation that I have just given. (p. 275)

Out of all of the accounts surveyed in this section so far, this account has the most going for it.[23] Of course, it wouldn't help us if what we are after is grounding robust political authority. And of course, one can question whether "rights" even make sense on purely naturalistic reasoning. Nonetheless, I do want to acknowledge Wolterstorff's account as a respectable account of political authority.

1.6 A Political Argument for God's Existence?

I hope to have shown thus far that, when it comes to secular accounts of political authority, each account seems to have major problems. Let's briefly recall them. Contractarian accounts seem susceptible to the charge that a subject's contract with the state is invalid due to there being no reasonable way to opt out. Moreover, contractarian accounts (hypothetical versions included) seem to have trouble with making sense of how the state has legitimate authority over explicit dissenters. Consequentialist accounts I took to be a bit more plausible though it wasn't clear to me whether consequentialist accounts are accounts of political authority. Assuming they are, it seems to me that, at best, consequentialist accounts can make sense of minimal political authority but not robust political authority. With respect to a naturalistic natural law account, my main criticism was that it's unlikely that you can make sense of teleology to the degree needed to make sense of genuine political obligation. And, finally, I argued that Wolterstorff's from "below" account, like the consequentialist account before it, at best (assuming you buy into rights talk), can only make sense of minimal political authority.

With respect to Wolterstorff's account from "above," I'm not aware of any significant obstacle in its way, at least outside of claiming that it is not probable that God exists. I imagine few people would question whether God, if He exists, could make sense of why states have authority. This especially seems to be the case if you already buy into the *possibility* of modified divine command ethics.[24] When I reflect on my seeming that leads me to believe that the state has robust political authority, and, when I commit myself to a phenomenological introspection of various stories that attempt to make sense of the seeming, the theory that the state derives its authority from God seems like a powerful explanation – at least if we are going to be realists about the nature of my seeming (i.e., if we aren't going to explain away the seeming by way of postulating unreliable intuitions).

---

[23] The account articulated here is similar to Daniel Laymen's Kantian-inspired account in Huemer and Layman (2021). Though I take it that Layman's account is weaker than Wolterstorff's account as Layman argues for the implausible view that only democracies possess legitimate authority. See page 81 for an example.

[24] For a defense of modified divine command theory, see Baggett and Walls (2011).

If I'm right about all of this, it seems we have modest evidence for God existence. Let's take the following as the evidence (E) to be explained: there are states that possess robust political authority. And let's call the hypothesis that God grants the state political authority the Political Argument for God hypothesis (PAG). We would surely expect E on PAG. And if what I have sketched is of any indication, we wouldn't expect to have E on −PAG.

Before I end this section, I'd like to conclude by briefly reconsidering natural law theory. However, instead of a naturalistic version, I'd like to consider a theistic one. It seems to me that God, as the creator of the parts that make us up (e.g., cognitive faculties), would be responsible for their design plans. We could make sense of how human nature and political philosophy are essentially teleological at its core. For God exists and He has given us the sort of natures that we have. This is roughly St. Thomas' 5th Way after all. Moreover, on the Aristotelian–Thomistic natural law theory, God's impartation to humans of the kind of nature that they have might in fact be part of the way that God grants authority to the state.

Having said all this, I see no reason why Wolterstorff's account should be seen as at odds with certain natural law theories. In fact, I think there are ways all such theories could complement each other. More on this for another day. I'm afraid our time is short. Moving on, I will now begin working with the idea that the state derives its authority from God. If the work here was too brief and not enough to convince you, I ask that you be a good chap and grant the view for the rest of this Element anyway. I'll now look at how God fits or could fit with popular frameworks in political philosophy.

2 God and Liberalism

2.1 God and Liberalism

Recall John Locke's social contract theory. John Locke endorsed the view that human beings are in a "*State of perfect Freedom* to order their Actions . . . as they think fit . . . without asking leave, or depending on the Will of any other Man" (Locke, 1960, p. 287). This is why, for Locke, we need to make a contract with the state before we have any obligations to obey it. It shouldn't be a surprise, then, that Locke was also a big advocate of property rights. Locke taught that we own our bodies. As an extension of owning our bodies, we own the work produced from our bodies.

> Though the earth, and all inferior creatures, be common to all men, yet every man has a property in his own person: this no body has any right to but himself. The labour of his body, and the work of his hands, we may say, are properly his. Whatsoever then he removes out of the state that nature hath

provided, and left it in, he hath mixed his labour with, and joined to it something that is his own, and thereby makes it his property. It being by him removed from the common state nature hath placed it in, it hath by this labour something annexed to it, that excludes the common right of other men: for this labour being the unquestionable property of the labourer, no man but he can have a right to what that is once joined to, at least where there is enough, and as good, left in common for others.

(Locke, 1980, sect. 27)

If I'm out and about and see a tree that doesn't belong to another subject, I can chop down the tree and turn that wood into a chair, or firewood, or a house. I'd own whatever comes from chopping down the tree as I earned it with my hard labor.

Now, there are two important caveats to make. First, as a Christian theist, Locke thought ultimately that God owns your body and that you are more like the primary keeper or renter of the body that you possess. Here, Locke can still be against legalizing suicide or endorsing other socially conservative laws. For, ultimately, God owns everything since everything is the product of God's effort. The second caveat is that Locke did put minimal restrictions on property rights when there is scarcity.

Nonetheless, when one takes God out of Locke's political philosophy, as professors teaching Locke typically do, we can see the groundwork for social liberalism. If God doesn't own our bodies, then only you own your body. You can do whatever you want with your body. There simply aren't any limits. Kiss who you want to kiss. Abort who you want abort. Do whatever makes you happy. You are your own.

Of course, for liberals like Locke and contemporary fusionists (i.e., those who fuse economic liberalism with social conservativism), this brand of liberalism is unfortunate and should be avoided. There remains to this day, however, a debate as to whether social liberalism is simply a natural and inevitable development (Deneen, 2018). We will touch on this in more detail in the following sections. As for now, we can unite liberals of all stripes by saying with John Stuart Mill that whenever there is debate about whether the state should endorse a coercive policy, "The *a priori* assumption is in favour of freedom" (Mill, 1963, p. 262).

2.2 The Different Strands of Liberalism and Their Critiques

While it's hard to imagine contemporary liberalism without Locke's influence, as alluded to briefly, there is a divide among liberals. On one hand, you have liberals who emphasize private property and private ownership and, on the other hand, you have liberals who emphasize the need for a larger state to protect and enforce rights, rights that usually include the right to healthcare, to food, and so on. Classical liberals want a minimal state while neoliberals prefer something closer to a welfare state. In order to explicate the views of the children of Locke, I will briefly survey the foremost thinker of each tradition.

Following Locke, Robert Nozick argues that human persons possess rights. A human person has the right to not be killed or harmed. A human person also has the right to develop his or her own conception of the good and follow it (Nozick, 1974, p. 49). A human person has these rights in part because they are

> [S]entient and self-conscious; rational (capable of using abstract concepts, not tied to responses to immediate stimuli); possessing free will; being a moral agent capable of guiding its behavior by moral principles and capable of engaging in mutual limitation of conduct; having a soul. (p. 48)

Nozick's philosophy is characterized by being a philosophy of noncoercion. Since Nozick views human rights as the sort of thing that can never be morally infringed by anyone or anything, a question emerges: How does the state possess authority over me?

Nozick tells an extremely elaborate justificatory story. It goes something like this: Imagine being in the state of nature. There are no governments, no police, and no military. What will people likely do? They will likely hire an agency for protection. Notice here, there is no taxation involved, especially taxation from income revenue. So it's not the case that an agency is coercing some individual to pay for its service. The individual's rights are respected and not infringed.

But surely, while there would initially be many agencies offering a degree of various services, one particular agency would come to dominate the market of protection agencies (p. 17). Let's call the agency that dominates the industry A1. Let's call some weaker rival of A1 A2. What happens when there is a dispute between subjects S1 and S2 when S1 pays for A1's service but S2 instead is a customer of A2? As the most competent agency, A1 has the best means to carry out justice. But, when adjudicating complaints about violations, Nozick thinks, we should always utilize the least error-prone or least risky method available. In this case, it would mean that A1's resources should be used over A2's. But this seems unfair to S2.

Surely A1 will tend to favor its costumer over a nonpaying client. So what should the state do? Nozick responds:

> It might be objected that either you have the right to forbid these people's risky activities or you don't. If you do, you needn't compensate the people for doing to them what you have a right to do; and if you don't … you ought simply to stop [the forbidding]. But the dilemma, "either you have a right to forbid it so that you needn't compensate, or you don't have a right to forbid it

so you should stop," is too short. It may be that you do have a right to forbid an action but only provided you compensate those to whom it is forbidden.

(p. 83)

In this case, A1 will provide a service to S2 as A1 prevents S2 from utilizing her protection agency. A1 now has a new customer that she must also represent. And here we have the explanation for how a state begins to emerge without illegitimate coercion. Once A1 represents all those in the geographical area and forces the other protection agencies to not utilize their methods of carrying out justice, she becomes a state. It's a minimal state, but it is a state. She is there only for the protection of rights and the enforcement of contracts.

So what should the theist think about Nozick's elaborate story? Well, first, the vast majority of theists share a seeming that leads them to believe that the state has more robust authority than what Nozick's account gets you. Red flags should come up immediately when considering Nozick's account. Moreover, if what I have argued for in Section 1 is right, we have reason to reject Nozick's view. Grounding political authority in God is a more plausible account of political authority than the hypothetical account Nozick gives. God grants the state robust authority to pursue the common good of society. The state has the authority to build a culture for its citizens, fund space exploration, legislate morality, and so forth. Nozick is simply wrong. The state has the right to do more than protect rights and enforce contracts. While Nozick's philosophy is right to promote human rights and to emphasize the state's responsibility to protect its citizens, it seems to me that theists who find themselves believing that the state possesses more robust authority will have good reason to reject Nozick's political philosophy.

What about John Rawls and the neoliberalism tradition? Should the theist make serious use of this political framework? Rawls asks his readers to imagine being behind a "veil of ignorance" where all members of a society can choose what rules they will be governed by. Now, here is the catch. If you are one of these members, you don't know what religion you will identify with, how much money you will have, what sort of handicaps you will possess, and so on. What sort of rules would you want to be governed by? Without knowing which conception of good you will likely endorse, if you are reasonable you will be led to think dogmatic religious beliefs shouldn't have a place in political legislation (Rawls, 2009, pp. 15–18). Rather, two guiding principles will emerge. First, each person has the equal right to the most extensive system of liberty available (p. 53). Second, the society would endorse what is known as the difference principle. Roughly the idea is that inequalities in legislation and political structure are permissible, iff, the inequalities involved would make it such that the least well off benefit the most (p. 53).

You can see the groundwork laid out for a secular state with wide-ranging authority. Wouldn't you want healthcare to be a right if you were behind the veil? You should support healthcare as a right. Wouldn't you want welfare and other robust distributive policies to be in place in case your luck isn't so good once the veil is opened? Then you should support a welfare state. And, again, if you don't want to suffer from religious discrimination, then you shouldn't support policies that discriminate against people who don't share your conception of the good. Humans have rights, and, if you're reasonable, you realize that you need a government with a far-reaching capacity to protect rights and establish fairness.

Now, you might be inclined to think Rawls is right. I mean, what happens once the veil is torn and it turns out that you're an atheist? You wouldn't want the state to endorse religion in any way, right? I'm not sure that's the case. Right now, because my argument in Section 1 is so convincing, let's say that you're a theist. And as a theist, you plausibly think that the most important part of life is having a right relationship with your creator and aiding your neighbors in their relationship with the creator. Let's assume for argument's sake that you are, objectively speaking, right about this too. Whether it is true or not, then, doesn't change if you happen to be an atheist tomorrow. In fact, for your own benefit, if you turned out to be an atheist when the veil is no longer in place, you would want the state to promote and teach theism as this might aid you in your own spiritual evolution. It might provide you with more resources for your own doxastic formation, leading you from belief that atheism is true to belief that theism is true. So it seems to me that Rawls is wrong.

Moreover, it's not clear to me how we should understand what Rawls means by "reasonable." Perhaps he means something like the following:

(RD) S is reasonable, iff, S is reasoning in accordance with the proper function of her cognitive faculties.

Plantinga endorses this as an account of rationality (Plantinga, 2000, chapter 4). If S is designed to produce the belief that her husband is in front of her, and S's cognitive faculties are functioning properly when S encounters her husband, we would say that S is being reasonable when she forms the belief that her husband is in front of her. That is, S is reasoning in accordance with her design plan. If, instead of S forming the belief that her husband is in front of her, she formed the belief that Thanos from the Marvel Cinematic Universe is in front of her, she could be said to be unreasonable.

Reasonability is determined by cognitive proper function. But what if Plantinga is right in that humans are designed to naturally produce the belief that Divinity exists (Plantinga, 2000)?[25] Assuming S's faculties are functioning properly when she forms the belief that Divinity exists, her belief would be reasonable. And, of course, pursuing interests related to the desires of God and reorienting her life to reflect the existence of God would all be reasonable things to do. In fact, it is epistemically possible that, due to the proper function of her faculties, she forms the belief that the state needs to conform in accordance with God's interests too. Can't we all conceive that there is a possible world where all of this is reasonable? This would seem to be at odds with a Rawlsian view of the state.

In the neoliberalism literature today, inspired by Rawls, there is a view known as public reason liberalism.[26] Roughly, its thesis is that, in order for a coercive policy to be justified, most or all of the members of the community must have an adequate or sufficient reason for enacting the policy (Vallier, 2014). On public reason liberalism, members of the society must have access to the reasons that justify a specific coercive policy. As Kevin Vallier puts it, "[P]ublic reason liberals must embrace justificatory internalism about reasons. If not, we cannot plausibly claim that these reasons are rationally recognizable, as agents may lack the psychological access to the relevant reasons" (pp. 104–105).

There are at least three specific traditions within the larger public reason view. First up is the public shared reason view (PSR). In defining this view, Vallier states, "A's reason RA can figure into justification for (or rejection of) a coercive Law L only if it is shared by all members of the public" (p. 110). This is obviously too demanding and unrealistic. There is very little, if anything at all, that will be agreed upon by everyone in a society.

On the opposite end of the spectrum is what is called convergence theory. For the convergence theory proponent, a reason is accessible and thus intelligible "for members of the public if and only if members of the public regard RA as epistemically justified for A according to A's evaluative standards" (p. 106). In this case, a Christian could rightfully appeal to scripture when she supports the state's ban on human abortion and a Unitarian Universalist could also appeal to her faith to support a policy that makes human abortion legal.

In between the convergence and PSR views is the view known as public reason accessibilism (PRA). A reason R is accessible, iff, members of the public take R to be justified according to a commonly held evaluative method (Vallier, 2014, p. 108). This leads Vallier to give what he calls the accessibility requirement:

---

[25] This seems to be well supported by cognitive science of religion. See Barrett (2011).
[26] I discuss this as well in McNabb (forthcoming).

Accessibility Requirement: A's Reason R can figure into a justification for (or rejection of) a coercive law L only if it is accessible to all members of the public. (p. 108)

This all seems right in line with Rawlsian reasoning. Reasonable people only want to use reasons that are accessible to all members in the community. Again, so the idea goes, you wouldn't want nonpublicly accessible reasons used to justify coercive legislation after the veil opens up. For it could be the case that you will lack access to such reasons.

Vallier develops a challenge for accessibilists, however. Roughly, the idea is that, if we define common evaluative standards too broadly, accessibilism will be compatible with religious reasons justifying legislation. This makes accessibilism no better than convergence theory. Thus, this option won't seem palatable for most public reason liberals. If, however, accessibilists define one's common evaluative standards too restrictively, then accessibilists won't be able to permit legislation that finds its justification in the testimony of perceived experts. Regarding the first point, Vallier argues that religious philosophers could use technical philosophical argumentation to conclude that God exists and then use this conclusion to argue for specific policy measures (p. 113).[27] Moreover, she might also use what she perceives to be reliable testifiers to conclude that some specific religious tradition is true. From here, she can argue from this religious doctrine that one should or shouldn't support specific legislation (p. 118). Regarding the other horn of the dilemma, Vallier argues that, if the accessibilist refuses to permit sophisticated philosophical argumentation and testimony as accepted methods of evaluation, then she will likely lose most of her justification for the policies she endorses. The clearest illustration of this rests in the climate change debate. Few people know the science behind climate change. Our legislators then, rely on the testimony of expert scientists to create policy. If we no longer permit testimony as a method of evaluation, then our climate change policy would be reduced to ashes.

So it seems to me not only that Rawls' political framework should be shunned if you're a theist, but the theist should also shun most contemporary Rawlsian political philosophy as well. Here's another reason I give in my forthcoming article, 'A Plantingian Response to Public Reason Accessiblism' (McNabb, forthcoming). In the world of biblical higher criticism, there are different schools of thought as it pertains to the historical Jesus enterprise. One school of thought, known as the Troeltschian tradition, argues that, when determining what the historical Jesus said and did, actual miracles should be ruled out.

---

[27] For example, see Craig and Moreland (2012), Swinburne (2004), Walls and Dougherty (2018), Corradini, Galvan, and Lowe (2010), and Feser (2017).

The Duhemian school, on the other hand, says that, before investigating the historical Jesus, we should set aside all beliefs that are at odds with what the consensus scholarship affirms. Plantinga disagree with both schools. Instead, Plantinga argues that, if one really has knowledge that Christianity is true, one shouldn't handicap themselves in their scriptural investigation (Plantinga, 2010, pp. 152–174). Why should the religious person handicap herself simply because other methodological approaches have asked her to? I find Plantinga's point compelling. Stating this, I think we can develop an even stronger argument against the Rawlsian political philosopher.

Public reason accessibilism of the Rawlsian stripe we are discussing can lead to obligatory self-harm. Now, to be clear, I don't think handicapping oneself is necessarily wrong. For example, if I were playing basketball against Luka Doncic of the Dallas Mavericks, I wouldn't consider it wrong if Luka spotted me a few extra points or if he decided to only shoot with his off hand. Nonetheless, we can think of situations where it would be impermissible for Luka to handicap himself. For example, if a multibillionaire pledged to give a million dollars to the homeless if Luka beats his opponent and the billionaire wouldn't give any money to the homeless if Luka loses, Luka would have a moral obligation to use everything within his power to win.

In what follows, I want to develop cases where handicapping oneself causes not only self-harm but harm to one's society. Before I make my point that accessibilism leads to self-harm being obligated for some religious persons, I want to make clear that, in part, my argument assumes the Aristotelian view that humans are social animals. In fact, in order to flourish as the sort of creatures that we are, we need relationships. Our flourishing depends in part on our society flourishing (Besong, 2018, p. 54). To arbitrarily break off a close friendship or cause harm to one's fellow citizens is to in turn cause harm to oneself. Assuming that Aristotle is right (because he is), what happens in a society will have a bearing on our own happiness.

Now, for the sake of argument, assume that pro-life persons are correct in that the institutionally approved killing of prenatal humans causes great destruction to a society. Let's also say that there is a religious subject S who has a justified belief that human abortion would cause great harm to her society; however, she isn't aware of nonreligious reasons for thinking so. If S is a convinced accessibilist, it seems she'd be obligated to commit self-harm. She'd be forced to handicap her knowledge and make decisions entirely based on secular reasons. Yet, when she advocates for the legalization of abortion, she would be perverting her own happiness and the happiness of those around her. This seems to be a reductio to accessibilism. In contrast, it seems reasonable and right for the religious subject to instead advance policies that protect prenatal humans.

Now, let's say that you committed to the pro-choice cause and this scenario doesn't move you much. If anything, you welcome the consequence of accessibilism. The state should not be in the business of protecting prenatal humans, or so you could think. It's not hard to imagine other scenarios where a religious subject has a justified, true belief about an ethical proposition that you support, but the subject's justification is only grounded in reasons that are religious in nature. And if the accessibilism of the sort we have been talking about is true, because her justification is purely religious in nature, she would be obligated to do other than what she knows. Here's another example:

> Sally lives in rural Texas and she is unfamiliar with the academic literature on climate change. In contrast to the contemporary academic literature, upon listening to a radio station that she trusts, she comes to believe that most secular folk think that climate change is a hoax and we can treat the earth in whatever way we want. Perhaps the radio station she listened to even cited fake academic papers that support that the earth always recovers from whatever people do to it. Nonetheless, Sally is religious and is convinced by her reading of Genesis that she should take care of the earth. This leads her to do things like recycle and protest businesses that come into town that don't seem to act in a manner that is compatible with her reading of Genesis.

Sally lacks secular reasons to support legislation that would ban businesses from being able to exploit the environment, but it seems wrong that she shouldn't be active in trying to save the environment. Again, an accessibilism that isn't compatible with religious reasons justifying coercive policy is at odds with what we intuitively think Sally should do. It seems right that we should either move away from a Rawlsian glossed accessibilism to another public reason view that is compatible with religion playing a role in public justification (i.e., endorse convergence theory), or we should totally reject public reason liberalism.

But I'm not too hopeful when it comes to convergence theory. It seems very much out of line with mainstream liberalism, and I think for good reason. Recall that many neoliberals find their inspiration in the work of Rawls and in the fact that reasonable people shouldn't support coercive laws on persons who don't share their conception of the good. This would be an impediment on the freedom that liberals wish to preserve. Convergence theory seems at odds with all of this and, in a sense, at odds with the liberal tradition. If it is genuinely a form of liberalism, it's a strand of liberalism that is immune from at least some of the criticism addressed here.

One final but brief criticism that I want to raise against liberalism simpliciter is more thoroughly explicated in Patrick Deneen's work *Why Liberalism*

Failed.[28] Deneen argues that liberalism leads to exploitation. As stated at the beginning of this section, liberalism is centered on maximizing freedom. We should support laws that are compatible with determining our own conception of happiness. We should be free to pursue the lifestyle of our choice. For example, if I want to have sex with whoever I want, I should be able to pursue that. Even if this lifestyle leads on the creation of prenatal humans. I shouldn't let prenatal humans get in the way of my freedom. The state legalizing abortion on demand, then, will be seen as vital to the human right to pursue one's own conception of the good life (Deneen, 2018, p. 39).

Similarly, we can see how this line of reasoning can lead to the exploitation of the planet (pp. 14–15). The state should endorse laws maximizing one's freedom to make money. If cutting down rainforests, fracking for oil, and polluting the ozone are required, then so be it. The state should get out of the business of telling its citizens how they can run their companies.

To make clear, Deneen is not arguing that there can't be liberals who are pro-life or pro-environment. Rather, the idea is that human exploitation and environmental exploitation is a likely consequence for a society whose primary desire for the state is for the state to maximize freedom. I'm fully willing to concede that individual liberty should be built into the state's conception of the good; it is in the interest of the state to emphasize the freedom of its citizens. However, a conception of the good that is limited to freedom, or something near about, is plausibly breeding grounds for exploitation of the worker, the human person, and the planet. The theist should not look favorably at these consequences as this is clearly not what God has intended. The theist disinterested in displeasing God might then be disinterested in liberalism altogether.

One political framework is especially concerned with exploitation: Marxism. Marxism can be seen as a reactionary theory to liberalism and, as such, it offers the theist a genuine alternative. Having looked at what liberalism has to offer the theist, we turn to critically engage a Marxist political framework.

3 God and Marxism

3.1 God and Marxism

In response to free markets creating inequalities among various persons and countries, the philosophy of Karl Marx emerged and took the world by storm. For the purposes of this Element, we can understand Marxism as the political thesis that, so long as capitalist systems and their influence remain, we should endorse revolutionary socialism until the state, material scarcity, and divisions

---

[28] Deneen (2018).

within labor cease to be.[29] That is, the Marxist thesis shouldn't be understood as interchangeable with the thesis of socialism, which I take to be a normative thesis about the state controlling the means of production. While Marxism endorses the use of socialist economic theory, socialism is seen as a means to an end rather than as an end in itself. Socialist philosophy is useful insofar as it enables the community to reach the next Hegelian development where the state ceases to be. Marx makes the distinction between his philosophy and socialism clear:

> In a higher phase of communist society, after the enslaving subordination of the individual to the division of labor, and therewith also the antithesis between mental and physical labor, has vanished; after labor has become not only a means of life but also life's prime want; after the productive forces have also increased with the all-round development of the individual, and all the springs of cooperative wealth flow more abundantly – only then can the narrow horizon of bourgeois right be crossed in its entirety and society inscribe on its banner: from each according to his ability, to each according to his needs. (Marx, 1974, pp. 323–325)

Now, you might be wondering why I am surveying a Marxist framework in an Element on God and political philosophy. Isn't Marxism incompatible with theism? Marx was, of course, no friend of religion. But it would be wrong to suggest that Marxism is incompatible with theism or even organized religion. Marxism isn't inherently secular. As Roland Boer puts it, "It is not so much that Marxism is either a secular or anti-secular programme, but it lies between these two possibilities. Marxism is engaged in perpetual negotiation, a dialectic if you like, between rejecting and refusing the world of capitalism and struggling with in it" (Boer, 2011, p. 30). In fact, Marx thought that enlightened humanity had moved past the whole theist and atheist debate. Roer tells us that Marx thought that atheism was a "distraction from the real task of communist analysis and action" (Boer, 2014, p. 49). In part, this is why Marx states that "Atheism . . . has no longer any meaning, for atheism is the negation of God, and postulates the existence of man through this negation; but socialism as socialism, no longer stands in need of such a meditation" (Marx, 1964, p. 145).

So Marx wasn't a committed evangelist for atheism and the minimal definition of Marxism given here isn't explicitly inconsistent with theism. But isn't Marxism opposed to religion given that Marxist regimes are known for persecuting religious believers? This assumption is misplaced. Marx was clear that violence against religion is "nonsense" (H., 1879). He thought that religion

---

[29] This definition takes the Marxist distinction from Arnold (2022) and combines it with Turner's (1975) informal definition.

would eventually cease, but it would do so nonviolently and as the result of socialism's growth. At the end of the day, however, philosophical Marxists generally hold that private beliefs don't matter. What matters is that "you are dedicated to the socialist cause" (Turner, 1975, p. 245). What matters more than being "orthodox" in one's belief system is that one has the right actions that contribute to the socialist revolution. What matters is correct praxis (p. 245).

In fact, Marx endorsed a radical view of freedom of conscience. He critiqued contemporary forms of liberalism for not going far enough with respect to freedom of religion (Boer, 2014, pp. 57–58). He thought that Western liberal traditions still made it hard to worship as you please, at least, if you weren't already a Christian. Roer summarizes Marx's critique well:

> For it sets up freedom only within the limited possibilities of a capitalist situation. In this light, freedom of religion will only ever mean certain types of acceptable religion, or for that matter political options. By contrast, a radical freedom of conscience transgresses such a limited approach by asserting the full range of choices, above all the one that changes the coordinates of the situation in which freedom of conscience was initially promulgated. (p. 60)

So, if the conflict between Marxism and theism isn't with respect to some inherent atheistic tenet that Marxism endorses, where does the conflict really lie? Denys Turner, from a Christian, specifically Catholic, perspective, tackles the question of whether Marxism is compatible with what the Chatholic Church teaches. His 'Can a Christian Be a Marxist?' primarily engages two objections. The first objection can be summarized as follows:

(1) The Church's teaching is incompatible with a materialist view of the world.
(2) Marxism entails a materialist view of the world.
(3) Therefore, the Church's teaching is incompatible with Marxism (Turner, 1975, p. 245).

Turner is quick to point out there is an obvious equivocation here. Regarding (2), the materialist view of the world entailed by Marxism pertains to a historical and materialist conception of human history. That is, there is an endorsement of some kind of causal closure principle. Something like the following: Behind every event in human history is a complete and sufficient explanation of that event, an explanation that reduces to the social relationships between humans. As Turner puts it, a materialist conception of history asserts that "all ontologies, Christian ontologies not excluded, are derived from, are formed, given content and force by the constraints of material human social relationships; that social relationships are embodiments of ideas and that, vice versa, all ideas, including abstract ontologies, are ideological transformations of a material social relationship" (p. 247).

This has nothing to do with what (1) is in reference to; (1) relates to the ontology of ultimate reality. The Church's teaching that there is a supernatural or immaterial aspect to ultimate reality is indeed incompatible with ontological materialism, but it isn't incompatible with what Marxists mean by materialism. Of course, you might understand Marxism differently. Perhaps you think that Marxism does entail a more ontologically robust materialism. If so, then indeed Marxism is incompatible with theism. If that is your view, then feel free to see the following discussion about what we can call soft Marxism or perhaps Marxism*.

For Turner, Christian Marxists are overdeterminationists. They believe that human history can be explained sufficiently by material embodied social relations. This will include why people believed in Christianity and even why people embrace Marxism. Nonetheless, it can be said that God has guided the historical process and God can be said to also sufficiently explain why people believe in Christianity or why people believe in Marxism (pp. 248–249). I imagine Turner could explain miracles in a similar fashion. Take the plagues surrounding the Exodus as an example. There could be sufficient explanations for the plagues that don't involve postulating the supernatural. Let's imagine that the plagues can be accounted for in purely physicalist terms. Nonetheless, at the end of the day, God is responsible for bringing about the naturalistic events about at just the right time such that we can say that God is ultimately the sufficient cause of the Exodus event.

The next objection Turner engages can be summarized as follows:

(1)   The Church's teaching is incompatible with revolutionary politics.
(2)   Marxism endorses revolutionary politics.
(3)   Therefore, the Church's teaching is incompatible with Marxism.

Contra the syllogism, Turner argues that "It's not true that the church is always against revolution but that it fragments itself over revolution or reaction" (pp. -248–249). I think what Turner means is that the Church's teaching can't be contained in the category of revolution or even in the category of reaction to revolution. The Church's teaching transcends these categories and yet informs both revolution and reaction. The overall trajectory of the Church, however, is marching forward to make itself obsolete. Just like Marxists look forward to the day when Marxism is no longer needed, the Church is on a path to abolish itself. Turner makes this point clear:

> I thus believe, both of Christianity and of Marxism, that, as historical praxes,
> they could not have anticipated their historical origins and that they will not

survive the completion of their historical tasks. I believe, with Marx, that both will realise themselves by abolishing themselves and abolish themselves in the act of their own realisation. (p. 249)

When the Church ushers in the eschaton, there will be no more need for the Church; there will be no need for sacraments or priests. In doing so, all the harm caused by the Church through any oppressive, racist, or abusive behavior will come to an end (p. 250). This seems consistent with both Christian belief and revolutionary politics.

Turner doesn't stop here, however; after showing that Marxism is compatible with theism, specifically Christianity, Turner goes on the offensive and argues that Christianity entails Marxism. Christians are called to love God and their neighbor; capitalism destroys our neighbor. We therefore must abolish capitalism through the realization of ending class altogether (p. 250). How can those who read the Sermon on the Mount be okay with corporations exploiting hundreds, sometimes thousands of workers through low wages, poor working conditions, and often meaningless work? Turner would find it implausible that a wealthy country would force its citizens to go bankrupt in order to pay off hospital bills. This simply isn't Christian love.

Now, I should point out that the Catholic Church has officially condemned what theologians call Marxist or liberation theology.[30] I imagine here that Turner would deny that what the Church has condemned is what he means by Marxism. Though, as someone who has little sympathy for Marxism, I feel no need to defend Turner's project here.

I do, however, want to point out another area where it seems that Marxist philosophy meshes well with the theist's project. It is often popularly asserted that religion is the cause of most wars. In fact, if it wasn't for religion, so the objection goes, we wouldn't have the current upheaval, terrorism, and wars in the Middle East. If Christianity and Islam ceased to be, so would the wars.

Utilizing a Marxist conception of history, we can offer a powerful retort. Religion isn't the primary cause of the war on terror. Rather, for the Marxist, the war on terror is the result of two capitalistic societies clashing over oil. Roer perfectly sums up this point:

> Let me give one more example: the current struggle between a supposedly Christian West and Muslim East. Is this struggle due to irreconcilable differences between two religions, which are actually quite close to one another? Of course not, for the current Muslim opposition arises from a long history of

---

[30] See, for example, the document issued by the Catholic Church titled, "Instruction on Certain Aspects of the 'Theology of Revelation,'" which can be accessed here: www.vatican.va/roman_curia/congregations/cfaith/documents/rc_con_cfaith_doc_19840806_theology-liberation_en.html.

capitalist imperialism. Although I should add a caveat, for even though Muslim culture and religion offers an alternative paradigm to liberal ideology that goes hand and hand with capitalism, Muslims countries are fully immersed – indeed they are aggressive players – within capitalist economics ... The obvious example is that cheap energy source known as oil; since Muslim-majority countries happen to be located where most of the world's oil happens to be, and since the overdeveloped West needs that oil, conflict is bound to rise. (Boer, 2014, p. 36)

He goes on to suggest that, if Buddhists occupied these lands, it would be the Christian West and Buddhist East that would be at odds. Marxism, then, seems to have tools to respond to objections against religion. But should theists be Marxists?

3.2 A Critique

I think most theists would agree that, if God exists, God would want us to pass laws that enable the weakest among us to flourish. This, in part, is what is driving philosophers like Turner to say that Christianity entails radical social-ism. But does radical socialism really lead to the prosperity of the weakest among us?

Starting from around the year 1800, a handful of countries, including the United States, Canada, Britain, Germany, Switzerland, and Japan, became rapidly rich through economic growth, while all other countries continued on a predictable economic path.[31] In "Justice and the Wealth of Nations," Dan Moller surveys various explanations for why the Great Divergence happened. One such explanation is that these countries exploited other countries or people groups. That is, these countries got rich by way of colonialism and war.

Moller dismisses these ideas and, according to him, most economic historians do too (Moller, 2014, p. 107). Specifically with respect to colonialism, the revenues received from colonial projects were not actually that significant. In fact, these funds were just a fraction of what these countries earned from their overall internal revenue (pp. 95, 101). Moreover, as Moller argues, if the explanation is to be all encompassing, it will need wide scope. That is, it will need to explain not only why Britain and the United States became very wealthy but also why countries like Canada and Switzerland got rich (p. 102). So, on the hypothesis that the Great Divergence is the result of immoral colonialism and war, we would need to commit to the idea that Switzerland and Canada also participated in great moral depravity (p. 102). This is implausible. And, as Moller points out, even when countries like Germany and Japan participated in

---

[31] Moller (2014, pp. 95, 101).

imperial conquest, they did so in a "manifestly fitful, inept, and impecunious manner . . . no one thinks that Germany got rich by invading Namibia" (p. 107).

An alternative explanation for the Great Divergence relates to these nations moving away from mercantilist economic policies. That is, as the countries moved away from policies that incentivize the exportation of goods but disincentivize and restrict the importation of goods, to embracing free trade and freer markets, more wealth emerged. Bas van der Vossen and Jason Brennan describe how nations produce more wealth when trade has less restriction:

> Both imports and exports can play an important role in making countries prosperous, depending on the way their economies function at a given time. In the long run, people and countries get richer by being productive, making better goods, and making them cheaper. The trick with trade is to find forms of exchange that foster this. When foreigners make goods relatively more efficiently, it makes sense to import them. Exports are best when it's relatively more efficient to produce things at home.
>
> (Van der Vossen and Brennan, 2018, p. 58)

All of this seems at odds with the state controlling the means of production and setting strict regulations on trade and the markets. And, given that Marxism is committed to revolutionary socialism, at least for the time being, it seems Marxism would endorse a counterproductive economic view. Marxists want to help the poor. But, if what I've said is right, the way to do that is to open up markets and trade, not restrict them. Now, of course, there could be reasons to still put restrictions on the market, specifically if putting restrictions on the market would help the common good, such as by breaking up monopolies or making an important moral statement. However, as a general rule, freer markets seem to increase wealth, and this seems at odds with Marxist philosophy.

There could be other pressing reasons why theists shouldn't endorse Marxism. If the theist thinks that any plausible account of the common good needs to include the good of freedom, Marxism might be in tension with this as well. Marxism seems to downplay or minimize the good of freedom and thus it is limited in how it can develop its conception of the good.

4 God and Post(Pre)liberalism

4.1 God and Nationalism

We now turn our attention to surveying postliberal theories. What follows is not an exhaustive survey. Rather, I have chosen political frameworks that have created much discussion in the past few years. Our first postliberal theory is nationalism. We are currently in the midst of a global nationalist revival. Between the successful Leave Campaign in the United Kingdom and the

2016–2020 Trump presidency in the United States, nationalism has been winning. In fact, as I write this, there is strong momentum for Poland to follow the United Kingdom in reclaiming some of its national sovereignty and leaving the European Union. But what is nationalism? Is God a nationalist?

First, let's define what we mean by nationalism as even using the term *nationalism* is controversial. I take it that a minimalist nationalism view endorses the following two theses:

(1)   When legislating policy, the welfare of one's own nation takes priority over the welfare of all other nations.
(2)   When developing its culture, a nation should strive for and emphasize a shared identity.[32]

Why should we think (1) is plausible? Well, when it comes to my family, I always prioritize my family over other families and their welfare. And it's not just that I make sure that I feed my family first before I feed other families. Of course I do that, but I also make sure that my family is prospering before I attend to the needs of others. I make sure that they have clothes, education, internet access, and toys as well. If this seems right and just or perhaps even obligatory to you, then (1) should seem plausible to you.

Nationalists will often say that nations are essentially reduced to a various collection of families (Hazony, 2018, pp. 76–81). In this way, we should view other families within our own nation as a part of our extended family. And, if we put our individual families before the well-being of other families, wouldn't we also make our extended family a priority?

While I don't doubt that some will perceive this as controversial, (2) is likely to be seen as the most controversial thesis. When one emphasizes that a state should have a shared national identity, a charge of Nazism is not far off. Everyone in Nazi Germany needed to look the same way, share the same values, embrace the same hatred for non-Aryan people, and so on. If we too are concerned with emphasizing a shared national identity, we are, in a similar vein, fascists, or at least so the worry goes.

There's no need to conflate nationalism with fascism or racism. In shared national identity, the color of one's skin can and should be considered irrelevant (Hazony, 2018, p. 20). As Yoram Hazony points out, Israelis tend to be nationalists. The same is obviously true with respect to the people of Israel in the Hebrew Bible. Yet Israel is made up of people possessing various colors. What's emphasized rather is being Jewish, being an Israeli, and believing in the God of the Hebrew Bible.

---

[32] Compare Neilsen (1999, p. 9).

It seems implausible to me that theists, especially of the Abrahamic tradition, should consider nationalism as intrinsically immoral when God seems to have endorsed laws and rituals that gave the people of Israel a strong distinct national identity. Moreover, God seemed to encourage Israel to consider its own welfare before the welfare of other nations. Of course, Israel was called to welcome the sojourner and the stranger, but the Hebrew Bible is concerned much more with Israel's behavior and how God's people should act among each other.

Now, perhaps you don't like the minimalist nationalist thesis mentioned in this section. You think that, if any platform is worthy of the title of nationalist, the platform would have to include a rejection of trying to influence other nations and their conception of the good. Each nation should determine its own standards, practices, and beliefs apart from external interference.

Now, if this is what is meant by nationalism, there does seem to be tension between at least some traditional theistic traditions and nationalism. For instance, in the Islamic tradition, eschatological hope is found in the establishment of a global Islamic caliphate. The nations are called to submit to Allah and implement sharia law. Similarly, in Christianity, Jesus calls his followers to make disciples of all nations and to teach the nations what Jesus commanded. Like in Islam, nations are called to submit to God, specifically in Christianity they are called to "kiss the son." Even in the Lord's Prayer, Christians are commanded to pray for God's kingdom to become a reality on earth. In both of these traditions, believers are commanded to influence the nations to follow God and the conception of good determined by their religion. The nations can't simply develop their own conception of the good. There's clear objectivity here and nations risk judgment by not endorsing the right conception of good.

So where should we look next? Perhaps the religions mentioned here have their own conceptual resources to develop their own plausible political philosophy. Might it be that God fits most naturally in a religious political framework over secular ones?

4.2 Islamic Political Philosophy

Let's say that a theist should be committed to an objective conception of the good, and let's say she is also committed to the enterprise of getting other nations to accept that conception of the good. Might we endorse an Islamic political framework? In what follows, I briefly sketch out a standard Sunni political philosophy and then proceed to develop a brief criticism.[33]

The Islamic tradition overwhelmingly affirms that God gives political authority to the state (March, 2019, p. 18). We are obligated to obey the

---

[33] For a narrower Islamic political vision, see Harvey (2019).

state, at least insofar as the state is doing the bidding of God, and this includes following specific political offices such as the caliph. The caliph, of course, is the supreme religious and political leader of the Muslim world. He's the rightful successor to the prophet Muhammad. How do we know who is the rightful caliph? The consensus of the earliest Muslims, the hadith, and reason determine this (p. 28). To deny the existence of the caliph is to commit heresy. The caliph office is essential to Islamic theology.

Ideally, the office of caliph is held by a gentlemen scholar, someone who is wise in political matters, knows the Quran, the hadith, and the tafsir, and can rightly apply sharia. Though, it is important to note that theologians were often utilized as advisers to Islamic rulers, even the caliph had advisers. So, historically, the caliph might fall short of the ideal.

Nonetheless, when the caliph, or rulers more generally, apply sharia rightly, humans are able to flourish. While implementing sharia seems at first glance to put restrictions on human freedom, sharia is a precondition to genuine human freedom. It enables humans to not be slaves to vice, corporations, and injustice, to have the freedom to be truly human and pursue the good. Sharia entails the rejection of the private life of the citizen. All personal matters relate to the common good.

But what do we do in times when there is no caliph, such as now? Some consider that the community in some sense can play a caliph-like role (pp. 75–113). The consensus of faithful Muslims is infallible and binding on all. The community should, then, implement sharia and regulate society as an Islamic one if possible. While traditional Islamic philosophy is antithetical to liberal democracy, Islam is consistent with theodemocracy (p. 79). The rule of the people, following God (which consists of implementing sharia), is to be considered a just and permissible form of government. Modern-day Muslims, then, can endorse the democratic process; it is God approved.

Here's one reason one might not be inclined to endorse an Islamic political philosophy. One might not find Islam compelling. This could be due to a lack of evidence for its historical claims, such as Jesus didn't really die on a cross.[34] Or perhaps you aren't impressed with the moral character of Muhammad. You might also have issue with sharia more generally. Finally, you could also find other religious traditions more historically compelling. Regardless of the reason, you might find the political philosophy painted here a nonstarter.

Nonetheless, a theist who isn't committed to Islam might find compelling the overall political structure it endorses. The theist might think that there is something that is special that binds all theists together. Perhaps whatever all

---

[34] See Q4:157.

morally good theists can agree on regarding God and His relation to the state should be implemented in all societies. This might include general precepts such as the state needing to publicly acknowledge God as its authority. At the end of the day, even if we reject the view discussed here, I imagine that there is much to be learned from the Islamic philosophical tradition.

4.3 God and Integralism

Let's take a religious tradition now that I'm more familiar with, the Catholic Christian tradition. When it comes to developing and systematizing Catholic doctrine as it relates to the Church's relationship to the state, Catholics will appeal to various sources. Each source carries its own evidential weight. For example, an ecumenical council's definitive teaching on faith or morals, and *ex cathedra* statements by the pope establish infallible doctrine. Papal encyclicals and bulls, on the other hand, while they carry heavy evidential weight, under normal circumstances should not be seen as infallibly binding. Weaker evidential sources would include apostolic exhortations and sermons given by the pontiff. Even carrying weaker evidential weight would be private comments or interviews given by the pontiff. Whatever the Catholic should believe, her views need to be consistent with these sources and their hierarchical rank.

So what do these sources say about the Church's relationship with the state? *Unam Sanctam*, a papal bull from the fourteenth century, tells us that there are two swords, a spiritual sword and a material sword. The Church holds the spiritual sword (i.e., it can discipline its members) and the state possesses the material sword. We are told that, while the state and Church carry distinct swords, the state is ultimately subject to the Church and its influence. In fact, we read that "Both, therefore, are in the power of the Church, that is to say, the spiritual and the material sword, but the former is to be administered *for* the Church but the latter *by* the Church; the former in the hands of the priest; the latter by the hands of kings and soldiers, but at the will and sufferance of the priest" (Pope Boniface VIII, 1302; emphasis original)

A natural reading of the text is that the Church can utilize the state to bear the material sword for its purposes. This isn't the only document to seemingly endorse religious coercion. Following *Unam Sanctam*, the Church used the state to bring back into the fold those who were baptized but have since left the faith. The famous Catholic humanist Erasmus argued that baptism isn't sufficient to coerce an individual apostate. Rather, he recommended that, when a child gets to a certain age, she should be asked to renew her baptism vows. If she did, she could now be legitimately coerced by the state if she were to leave the faith. If not, there could be no punishment for her besides being barred from the sacraments. On one interpretation, the Council of Trent rejected Erasmus' proposal in very strong terms (Pink, Unpublished). The Council of Trent does this in Session 7 Canon 14:

> If anyone says that when they grow up those baptised as little children should be asked whether they wish to affirm what their godparents promised in their name when they were baptised; and that, when they reply that they have no such wish, they should be left to their own decision and not, in the meantime, be coerced by any penalty into the Christian life, except that they be barred from the reception of the eucharist and the other sacraments, until they have a change of heart: let him be anathema. (Alberigo and Tanner, 1990, p. 686)

Now, lest you be tempted to think that what's being discussed is simply the Church's view in the medieval era, let me assure you that the magisterium continued to express similar views at least until Vatican 2.[35] For example, Pope Leo XIII states in an encyclical that "the Church ... deems it unlawful to place the various forms of divine worship on the same footing as the true religion" (Pope Leo XIII, 1885). Pope Pius the IX states that:

> For you well know, venerable brethren, that at this time men are found not a few who, applying to civil society the impious and absurd principle of "naturalism," as they call it, dare to teach that "the best constitution of public society and (also) civil progress altogether require that human society be conducted and governed without regard being had to religion any more than if it did not exist; or, at least, without any distinction being made between the true religion and false ones." And, against the doctrine of Scripture, of the Church, and of the Holy Fathers, they do not hesitate to assert that "that is the best condition of civil society, in which no duty is recognized, as attached to the civil power, of restraining by enacted penalties, offenders against the Catholic religion, except so far as public peace may require." From which totally false idea of social government they do not fear to foster that erroneous opinion, most fatal in its effects on the Catholic Church and the salvation of souls, called by Our Predecessor, Gregory XVI, an "insanity," 2 viz., that "liberty of conscience and worship is each man's personal right, which ought to be legally proclaimed and asserted in every rightly constituted society; and that a right resides in the citizens to an absolute liberty, which should be restrained by no authority whether ecclesiastical or civil, whereby they may be able openly and publicly to manifest and declare any of their ideas whatever, either by word of mouth, by the press, or in any other way." (Pope Pius IX, 1864)

Similarly, Pope Pius IX states that rulers of nations who wish to preserve their authority and promote prosperity will not neglect their public duty of reverence

---

[35] For a clear medieval explication of why the state needs to submit to Christ and the Church, see Aquinas (2014).

and obedience to Christ. We are told that, once men recognize both privately and publicly Christ as king, society, "at last [will] receive the great blessings of real liberty, well-ordered discipline, peace and harmony." In fact, Pope Pius argues that the Church has a right to "teach mankind, to make laws, to govern peoples in all that pertains to their eternal salvation." Once that right was denied, the collapse of Western civilization occurred.

So it seems that the Catholic Church teaches that humans are governed by two distinct social communities – the state and the Church. While each has its own primary end and expertise, the Church can use the state to do some of its bidding, such as to promote Christianity and perhaps even to coerce apostates back into the faith. God, then, not only is responsible for giving states their authority (see Section 1), but He is also still intimately connected and active with the governments of the world. They are called to promote salvation and publicly submit to Christ as king. As the Psalmist says,

> Therefore, you kings, be wise;
> be warned, you rulers of the earth.
> Serve the LORD with fear
> and celebrate his rule with trembling.
> Kiss his son, or he will be angry
> and your way will lead to your destruction,
> for his wrath can flare up in a moment.
> Blessed are all who take refuge in him.[36]

All of this would seem uncontroversial to most Catholic theologians, at least until the mid-twentieth century, when some – let's call them abrogationists – see a departure from what the Church taught through the ordinary magisterium and what we see at Vatican 2. The idea is that, while the encyclicals and papal bulls referenced in this section were binding for a time, they were never part of the Church's infallible teaching. The Church, rather, infallibly spoke through the ecumenical council known as the Second Vatican Council and has made past non-infallible teaching obsolete or abrogated. Here, chapter six of *Dignitatis Humanae* is usually cited:

> The protection and promotion of the inviolable rights of man ranks among the essential duties of government. Therefore government is to assume the safeguard of the religious freedom of all its citizens, in an effective manner, by just laws and by other appropriate means ... If, in view of peculiar circumstances obtaining among peoples, special civil recognition is given to one religious community in the constitutional order of society, it is at the

---

[36] Psalms 2 (NIV).

same time imperative that the right of all citizens and religious communities to religious freedom should be recognized and made effective in practice. Finally, government is to see to it that equality of citizens before the law, which is itself an element of the common good, is never violated, whether openly or covertly, for religious reasons. Nor is there to be discrimination among citizens. (*Dignitatis Humanae*, 1965).

It looks like Vatican 2 is forbidding religious coercion. Even if the state recognizes a specific religion, we are told that the rights of the religious minority should be upheld and recognized. The Council demands equality for every citizen.

So, are those who advocate that the Church's endorsement of religious coercion has been rescinded (i.e., the abrogationists) correct? Thomas Pink thinks not. Pink argues that we should understand *Dignitatis Humanae* as addressing states who are not in communion with the Church. Moreover, Pink contends that we should understand the document as addressing the natural rights humans possess sans baptism. One should never be coerced to become a Christian. This would be a violation of natural law. But, once a subject becomes a Christian by baptism, the subject enters the Church's jurisdiction and the Church can now utilize the state to motivate the subject back to the faith if she ever commits apostasy (Pink, 2017, pp. 105–146). Again, the idea that the Church can use the material sword of the state goes back to *Unam Sanctam*.

Furthermore, on at least one interpretation, the Church made sure to anathematize the view that denied that a valid baptism was sufficient grounds to be religiously coerced. With the later papal encyclicals, we see that the Church has the right to "teach mankind, to make laws, to govern peoples in all that pertains to their eternal salvation." Political rulers should publicly submit to Christ's lordship and promote Christianity. It's through this that we are told states will possess permanent happiness and prosperity.

Some argue that, due to the longevity of the Church's teaching on these issues, the abrogationists are a bit too hasty. The more traditionally inclined will argue that we should not throw out what the Church has taught through its ordinary magisterium so quickly. It seems like something that should be done only as a last resort. It's much easier to simply accept Pink's reading of *Dignitatis Humanae*, or so they say. This all becomes even more apparent when we recognize that a fundamental principle in Catholic theology is that we should generally interpret new teaching as if it were consistent with previous teaching. Call this the hermeneutic of continuity. Call the view that is primarily being discussed in this section integralism. Vallier helpfully puts the thesis of integralism in schematic form:

Catholic Integralism affirms four principles:

(1) Natural Authority: God authorizes a state to advance the natural common good G of a community C.

(2) Supernatural Authority: God authorizes the church to advance the supernatural common good S of all baptized persons in C.

(3) Supernatural Sovereignty: to advance S, the church may mandate state policies P backed by civil penalties E that advance S directly (i.e., not merely by means of advancing G), without excessively undermining G (or S in some other respect).

(4) Catholic Society: integralism is an ideal for C iff C's observant Catholics form proportion I of C. (Vallier, forthcoming)

Hopefully there isn't a need to do too much explication as this is the view that has primarily been looked at in this section. Theses (1) and (2) simply claim that God has granted authority to the state to pursue the natural ends of its citizens and that God has also granted the Church authority to pursue the supernatural ends of its members. Those who took time to read Section 1 of this Element should be able to make sense of this well enough. Thesis (3) has been discussed at length in this section. Motivated in part by *Unam Sanctam* and the Council of Trent, the Church has the authority to use the state to invoke penalties on the baptized if the Church deems it necessary. And, finally, thesis (4) is a simple claim that these theses should be endorsed and implemented in those societies where it is possible.

So why shouldn't we all be Catholic integralists? Well, one objection, of course, would be that Catholicism is false. It could be said that there is some defeater for believing that the teachings of the Church are true. While I would love to invest time in defending the Holy Catholic and Apostolic Faith, I'm afraid this Element doesn't permit the room to engage this objection.[37] Instead, I'd like to look at a moral objection that someone who endorses Catholicism, or at least, someone who is open to Catholicism, might share. The argument goes something like this: I agree with Pink that it's much easier to contextualize *Dignitatis Humanae* than endorse the thesis endorsed by abrogationists. Nonetheless, it's better to endorse abrogationism or perhaps endorse alternative interpretations to the Church's previous social teaching, than to be committed to the view that it is permissible for the state to coerce its citizens in religious matters.[38] That is, the Catholic might say, that her seeming that leads her to believe that it's always impermissible for the state to coerce her subjects for

---

[37] For an epistemological defense of the Catholic Church, see McNabb and Baldwin (2020).

[38] For example, see John Finnis' interpretation of the canons of Trent in Finnis (2013).

religious reasons, is stronger than her seeming that leads her to believe that abrogationism is false.

I'd like to set out several thought experiments that I think might weaken the former seeming.

Coercion 1 (C1)

Your state enters into an official relationship with the Church. The Church directs your state to declare that Jesus is king and that the Catholic Church is the one true Church. As a result, millions more people will be saved from the torments of hell.

Coercion 2 (C2)

Your state has an official relationship with the Church. The Church directs your state to use tax money to fund the Catholic Church. As a result, millions more people will be saved from the torments of hell.

Coercion 3 (C3)

Your state has an official relationship with the Church. The Church directs your state to tax one cent to those who leave the faith. As a result, millions more people will be saved from the torments of hell.

Coercion 4 (C4)

Your state has an official relationship with the Church. The Church directs your state to restrict former Catholics from proselytizing those who belong to the Catholic Church. As a result, millions more people will be saved from the torments of hell.

Coercion 5 (C5)

Your state has an official relationship with the Church. The Church directs your state to restrict former Catholics from voting. As a result, millions more people will be saved from the torments of hell.

Is C1 problematic? If you're a Christian or Catholic, I'm not sure why it would come across as problematic. Matthew 28:19–20 states:

> Therefore go and make disciples of all nations, baptizing them in the name of the Father and of the Son and of the Holy Spirit, and teaching them to obey everything I have commanded you. And surely I am with you always, to the very end of the age.[39]

While this verse doesn't necessitate that states have a relationship with the Church, the verse fits comfortably with C1. Christians are called to advance Christ's kingdom. The Church is supposed to teach the nations the ways of God. If governments publicly declare that they are following Christ, would that really be a bad thing? Perhaps you are still uncomfortable with the idea of

---

[39] NIV translation.

even the most minimally invasive religious coercion. Let's reflect on this. Imagine that you are an orthodox Catholic Christian. Orthodox Catholics believe hell is a real place where suffering never ceases and where hatred reigns supreme. Imagine an eternity of suffering for not just one person but millions. Picture a person in hell. Do you see the anguish in their eyes? Can you begin to fathom their desperation? Are you able to comprehend their loneliness? Now, multiply this by millions. Are you still uncomfortable with the coercion involved in C1?

Let's say that you are now comfortable with C1. Is C2 going to make you uncomfortable again? Think about what the state does with your tax money and how it likely funds projects you disagree with. Would you really prefer that the state avoids using some of its revenue to aid the Church in its mission and, in turn, millions more die and go to hell?

Let's say you're still with me and you no longer have a problem with religious coercion simpliciter. Really what you are uncomfortable with relates to cases 3–5. It's really that you find the more robust scenarios of religious coercion problematic. But, again, think about these cases in light of millions of people being damned. Is your seeming that it's always wrong for a state to religiously coerce its citizens still strong? In case C3, we are talking about only penalizing former Catholics by one cent. In this possible world, doing this saves millions from hell.

While I don't mean to endorse a strictly consequentialist justification of religious coercion, I went through these cases in hopes to weaken the seeming that the reader might share that leads her to believe that the state should never coerce individuals for religious reasons. Of course, if you still think religious coercion is intrinsically wrong and intrinsically wrong actions can never be justified, these cases shouldn't move you. However, if you are undecided or if perhaps these cases have brought doubt to you that religious coercion is always wrong, then I take it that these thought experiments have served our purposes. Let me be clear: I am not here endorsing C1–C6. My goal is to merely motive the idea that religious coercion is not always wrong.

Of course, we could think of another scenario that harms our modern liberal sensibilities even more than scenarios 3–5. Your state has an official relationship with the Church. The Church determines that public figures who leave the Catholic faith and speak openly about it are to be sentenced to a nontrivial amount of time in prison. As a result, millions more people will be saved from the torments of hell.

I imagine that there has to be some threshold as to what the state could and should do to save souls and promote the one true Church. I don't pretend to offer some criteria that can help integralists with demarcation. Instead, as someone who endorses phenomenal conservatism about justification, I think integralists should be guided by their seemings as for what is too much. In a democratic country, one would rely on the overall seemings of those who voice their opinion in the voting booth. Nonetheless, I think the aforementioned scenarios will, on average, weaken one's confidence in thinking that it is always wrong for states to coerce citizens for religious reasons.

Let's say however, that you are convinced by the Church's nineteenth- and twentieth-century papal encyclicals that the state should promote Christianity for the spiritual well-being of its citizens, but you simply see the sort of religious coercion involved in cases 3–5 as morally problematic. We can call the minimal type of religious coercion involved in cases 1–2 coercion1 and the type of robust coercion in cases 3–5 coercion2. You might think that what *Dignitatis Humanae* is after is a condemnation of coercion2 and not coercion1. You then look at the Catholic texts that seem to endorse coercion2 and opt for alternative interpretations of these texts or endorse the abrogationist thesis. In this way, you can agree with relatively recent popes that the state should pursue the spiritual well-being of its citizens by becoming confessional, while at the same time you can be led by your strong seeming that it's impermissible for states to coerce2. We can call this view the minimalist integralist view. It's still integralist because you endorse that the state is subject to the Church and that we should strive for all states to eventually become confessional. Yet it doesn't have the strong antiliberal bite that comes with the integralism of people like Thomas Pink. Perhaps, in this way, the minimalist integralist can have her cake and eat it too. Of course, you might reject integralism altogether and have a different approach to political theory and religious faith. My mapping out political positions that theists or Catholics can hold should by no means be considered exhaustive. Nonetheless, I think what I have shown is that theists can and should pull from their religious traditions when formulating their political frameworks. They shouldn't formulate their political framework as secularists would. They have a wealth of resources at their disposal.

4.4 In Closing

Our journey is now coming to an end. It's now time to follow that redundant process of summarizing what we have explored and for me to make clear what really has been argued for. In Section 1, I surveyed contemporary secular accounts of political authority and argued that these accounts fail to make sense of how states possess what I called robust political authority. Instead, I proposed that we should take seriously the claim that God grants the state its authority. I then began a project of looking at various political frameworks and asked which framework fits best with theism.

In Section 2, I surveyed the liberal tradition. After this, I argued that both classical liberalism and neoliberalism should be seen as problematic for the theist. The former has issues with the political authority account given in Section 1. The latter has issues with religion in the public sphere. Moreover, I argued that most liberal theories should be avoided by committed theists because they entail implausible harmful handicaps against religious persons. With respect to those liberal theories that might avoid the criticisms raised here, I questioned whether they are really liberal theories. Finally, I argued that liberalism simpliciter is a breeding ground for exploitation of human life as well as exploitation of our planet. While I did raise criticisms against liberalism, I argued that any good political framework should take into account components of liberalism. As stated, we should view individual freedom as part of the state's conception of the good.

In Section 3, we spent time going over whether there is genuine conflict between Marxism and theism. I argued that there isn't necessarily conflict, but there is some deep concord. Theists should love their neighbor and not exploit him. We should hope classes cease in the eschaton and we should look forward to the day when the Church as we know it is no longer needed. Nonetheless, we should also note that free markets likely can and have brought many states out of poverty. While man was not made for the market and we shouldn't sacrifice man on the altar of GDP, a disposition to see freer markets more charitably seems warranted.

Finally, not being satisfied with the two main secular political frameworks of the twentieth century, we looked at three versions of what I called post-liberalism. First, we discussed the justification for buying into the minimalist nationalist thesis. Roughly, the argument was to draw a parody between the family and the collection of families we call a nation. If we think we first must take care of our family before we take care of our neighbor, then we should think that we should emphasize the well-being of our own nation before worrying about the well-being of other nations. However, I then looked at a more robust articulation of nationalism and argued that certain stripes of theists (such as Catholics and Muslims) would do well to avoid it as a nationalism that entails we should let the states determine their own conception of good is incompatible with orthodox Christianity and Islam. We then spent time looking at Islam and Christianity (specifically Catholicism) and explored resources these traditions offered us. While one might reject the total visions of these religious traditions, there are still things to be learned. If you are a convinced believer, however, it seems like the political framework that comes most natural to you should be the political framework that has historic roots with your tradition. While this goes against the liberal sensitivities ingrained in us since the Enlightenment, I tried to minimize some of the worry by reflecting on the supernatural goods that could be had if a state did become religious or supported policies that were motived by religion.

References

Alberigo, Norman Tanner. (1990). "*Council of Trent*, Session 7, Decree on Baptism, Canon 14, 3 March 1547." In *Decrees of the Ecumenical Councils*. Volume 2. Ed. Norman Tanner. London: Sheed and Ward, p. 684.

Aquinas, Thomas. (2014) *De Rengo*. Milwaukee, WI: Divine Providence Press.

Arnold, Samuel. "Socialism." *Internet Encyclopedia of Philosophy*. https://iep.utm.edu/socialis.

Baggett, David, and Jerry L. Walls. (2011). *Good God: The Theistic Foundations of Morality*. New York: Oxford University Press.

Baldwin, Erik, and Tyler Dalton McNabb. (2018). *Plantingian Religious Epistemology and World Religions*. Lanham, MD: Lexington Books.

Barrett, Justin L. (2011). *Cognitive Science, Religion, and Theology from Human Minds to Divine Minds*. West Conshohocken, PA: Templeton Press.

Bergmann, Michael. (2002). "Common Sense Naturalism." In *Naturalism Defeated?* ed. James Beilby. Ithaca, NY: Cornell University Press, 61–90.

Besong, Brian. (2018). *An Introduction to Ethics: A Natural Law Approach*. Eugene, OR: Cascade Books.

Boer, Roland. (2011). *Criticism of Religion: On Marxism and Theology*. Chicago, IL: Haymarket Books.

(2014). *In the Vale of Tears: On Marxism and Theology*. Leiden: Brill.

Pope Boniface VIII (1302). "Unam Sanctum." *Papal Encyclicals Online*. www.papalencyclicals.net/bon08/b8unam.htm.

Corradini, Antonella, Sergio Galvan, and E. J. Lowe. (2010). *Analytic Philosophy without Naturalism*. London: Routledge.

Craig, William Lane and J. P. Moreland. (2012). *The Blackwell Companion to Natural Theology*. Oxford: Wiley-Blackwell.

D'Agostino, Fred, and Gerald Gaus. (2021). "Contemporary Approaches to the Social Contract." *Stanford Encyclopedia of Philosophy*. https://plato.stanford.edu/entries/contractarianism-contemporary.

Deneen, Patrick J. (2018). *Why Liberalism Failed*. New Haven, CT: Yale University Press.

Dignitatis Humanae. (1965). www.vatican.va/archive/hist_councils/ii_vatican_council/documents/vat-ii_decl_19651207_dignitatis-humanae_en.html.

Dworkin, Ronald. (1986). *Law's Empire*. Cambridge, MA: Harvard University Press.

Feser, Edward. (2009). *Aquinas*. London: Oneworld.

(2017). *Five Proofs of the Existence of God*. San Francisco: Ignatius Press.

Finnis, John. (2011). *Natural Law and Natural Rights*. Oxford: Oxford University Press.

(2013). "John Finnis on Thomas Pink." In *Reason, Morality and Law: The Philosophy of John Finnis*, ed. John Keown and Robert George. Oxford: Oxford University Press, 566–577.

Foot, Phillipa. (2002). *Virtues and Vices*. Oxford: Oxford University Press.

H. (1879). "Interview with Karl Marx." *Chicago Tribune*, January 5.

Harvey, Ramon. (2019). *The Qur'an and the Just Society*. Edinburgh: Edinburgh University Press.

Hazony, Yoram. (2018). *The Virtue of Nationalism*. New York: Hachette.

Hsiao, Tim. (2017). "The Perverted Faculty Argument." *Philosophia Christi* 19: 207–216.

Huemer, Michael. (2001). *Skepticism and the Veil of Perception*. Lanham, MD: Rowman & Littlefield.

(2013). *The Problem of Political Authority*. Basingstoke: Palgrave Macmillan.

Huemer, Michael, and Daniel Layman. (2021). *Is Political Authority an Illusion?* London: Routledge.

Hume, David. (2009). *A Treatise of Human Nature*. Portland, OR: Floating Press.

Pope Leo XIII (1885). "Immortale Dei." *Papal Encyclicals Online*. www .vatican.va/content/leo-xiii/en/encyclicals/documents/hf_l-xiii_enc_ 01111885_immortale-dei.html.

Locke, John (1960). *Two Treatises of Government*. Ed. Peter Laslett. Cambridge: Cambridge University Press.

(1980). *Second Treatise of Government*. Ed. Crawford Brough McPherson. Indianapolis, IN: Hackett.

(1988). *Two Treatises of Government*. Cambridge: Cambridge University Press.

March, Andrew. (2019). *The Caliphate of Man*. Cambridge, MA: Harvard University Press.

Marx, Karl. (1964). *Economic and Philosophic Manuscripts of 1844*. New York: International.

(1974). "Critique of the Gotha Program." In *Marx and Engels Collected Works*. New York: International, pp. 79–94.

McNabb, Tyler Dalton. (2018). *Religious Epistemology*. Cambridge: Cambridge University Press.

(In Press). "A Plantingian Response to Public Reason Accessibilism." In *The Palgrave Handbook to Religion and State in the Western Hemisphere*, ed. Shannon Holzer.

McNabb, Tyler Dalton, and Erik Baldwin. (2020). "Religious Epistemology in Analytic Theology." In *T&T Clark Handbook of Analytic Theology*, ed. James Arcadi and James Turner. London: Bloomsbury Press, 33–44.

Mill, John Stuart. (1963). *Collected Works of John Stuart Mill*, ed. John M. Robson. Toronto: University of Toronto Press.

Miller, Fred. (1998). "Presuppositions of Aristotle's Politics." *Stanford Encyclopedia of Philosophy*, https://plato.stanford.edu/entries/aristotle-politics/supplement2.html.

Moller, Dan. (2014). "Justice and the Wealth of Nations." *Public Affairs Quarterly* 28/2: 95–101.

Murphy, Mark. (2017) *God's Own Ethics*. Oxford: Oxford University Press.

Neill, Jeremy, and Tyler Dalton McNabb. (2019). "By Whose Authority: A Political Argument for God's Existence." *European Journal of Philosophy of Religion* 11/2: 163–189.

Neilsen, Kai. (1999). "Cosmopolitanism, Universalism and Particularism in the Age of Nationalism and Multiculturalism," *Philosophical Exchange* 29: 3–34.

Nozick, R. (1974). *Anarchy, State, and Utopia*. New York: Basic Books.

Pink, Thomas. (2017). "*Dignitatis Humanae*: Continuity after Leo XIII." In *"Dignitatis Humanae Colloquium" Dialogos*. Volume 1, ed. Thomas Crean and Alan Fimister. Aurora, CO: Dialogos Institute, 105–146.

(Unpublished). "John Finnis' Alternative History of Trent." www.academia.edu/37861294/John_Finniss_Alternative_History_of_Trent.

Pope Pius IX. (1864). "Quanta Cura." *Papal Encyclicals Online*. www.papalencyclicals.net/pius09/p9quanta.htm.

Plantinga, Alvin. (1993). *Warrant and Proper Function*. New York: Oxford University Press.

(2000). *Warranted Christian Belief*. New York: Oxford University Press.

(2010). *Where the Conflict Really Lies: Science, Religion, and Naturalism*. New York: Oxford University Press.

(2012). "Darwinist Materialism Is Wrong." *The New Republic*. https://newrepublic.com/article/110189/why-darwinist-materialism-wrong.

Rawls, John. (2009). *A Theory of Justice*. Cambridge, MA: Harvard University Press.

Salzillo, Raphael. (2021). "The Mereology of Thomas Aquinas." *Philosophy Compass* 16/3: 1–10.

Sandeford, David. (2018). "Organizational Complexity and Demographic Scale in Primary States." *Royal Society Open Science*. **5**: 171–237.

Skalko, John. (2019) *Disordered Actions*. Neunkirchen, Germany: Editones Scholasticae.

Swinburne, Richard. (2004). *The Existence of God.* Oxford: Oxford University Press.

Tollefsen, Deborah. (2007). "Group Testimony." *Social Epistemology* 21: 299–311.

Turner, Deny. (1975). "Can a Christian Be a Marxist?" *New Black Friars* 56: 244–253.

Vallier, Kevin. (Forthcoming). *All the Kingdoms of the World.* Oxford: Oxford University Press.

2014. *Liberal Politics and Public Faith: Beyond Separation.* New York: Routledge.

Van der Vossen, Bas, and Jason Brennan. (2018). *In Defense of Openness: Why Global Freedom Is the Humane Solution to Global Poverty.* New York: Oxford University Press.

Waldron, Jeremy. (1999). *Law and Disagreement.* Oxford: Oxford University Press.

Walls., Jerry L., and Trent A. Dougherty. (2018). *Two Dozen (or so) Arguments for God: The Plantinga Project.* Oxford: Oxford University Press.

Wolterstorff, Nicholas. (2012a). "Accounting for Political Authority of the State." In *Understanding Liberal Democracy.* Ed. Nicholas Wolterstorff and Terence Cueno. Oxford: Oxford University Press.

(2012b). *The Might and the Almighty.* Cambridge: Cambridge University Press.

Acknowledgments

I'd like to thank my wife and kids for letting me work on this Element, especially since most of this was written when we were quarantined in Hong Kong. I love you, Priscilla, Eden, Elijah, Ezra, Eva-Maria, and Ezekiel. On a similar note, I'd like to thank the creator of *Fortnite* as the game permitted me to write with only a few interruptions. I also want to thank Michael DeVito, who endured the painful hardship of reading this Element. I'm grateful for your feedback.

Cambridge Elements ≡

The Problems of God

Michael L. Peterson
Asbury Theological Seminary
Michael Peterson is Professor of Philosophy at Asbury Theological Seminary. He is the
author of *God and Evil* (Routledge); *Monotheism, Suffering, and Evil* (Cambridge University
Press); *With All Your Mind* (University of Notre Dame Press); *C. S. Lewis and the Christian
Worldview* (Oxford University Press); *Evil and the Christian God* (Baker Book House); and
Philosophy of Education: Issues and Options (Intervarsity Press). He is co-author of *Reason
and Religious Belief* (Oxford University Press); *Science, Evolution, and Religion: A Debate
about Atheism and Theism* (Oxford University Press); *and Biology, Religion, and Philosophy*
(Cambridge University Press). He is editor of *The Problem of Evil: Selected Readings*
(University of Notre Dame Press). He is co-editor of *Philosophy of Religion: Selected Readings*
(Oxford University Press) and *Contemporary Debates in Philosophy of Religion*
(Wiley-Blackwell). He served as General Editor of the Blackwell monograph
series Exploring Philosophy of Religion and is founding Managing Editor of the
journal *Faith and Philosophy*.

About the Series
This series explores problems related to God, such as the human quest for God or gods,
contemplation of God, and critique and rejection of God. Concise, authoritative volumes
in this series will reflect the methods of a variety of disciplines, including philosophy of
religion, theology, religious studies, and sociology.

Cambridge Elements ☰

The Problems of God

CPSIA information can be obtained
at www.ICGtesting.com
Printed in the USA
LVHW021035100523
746600LV00010B/644

9 781009 269100